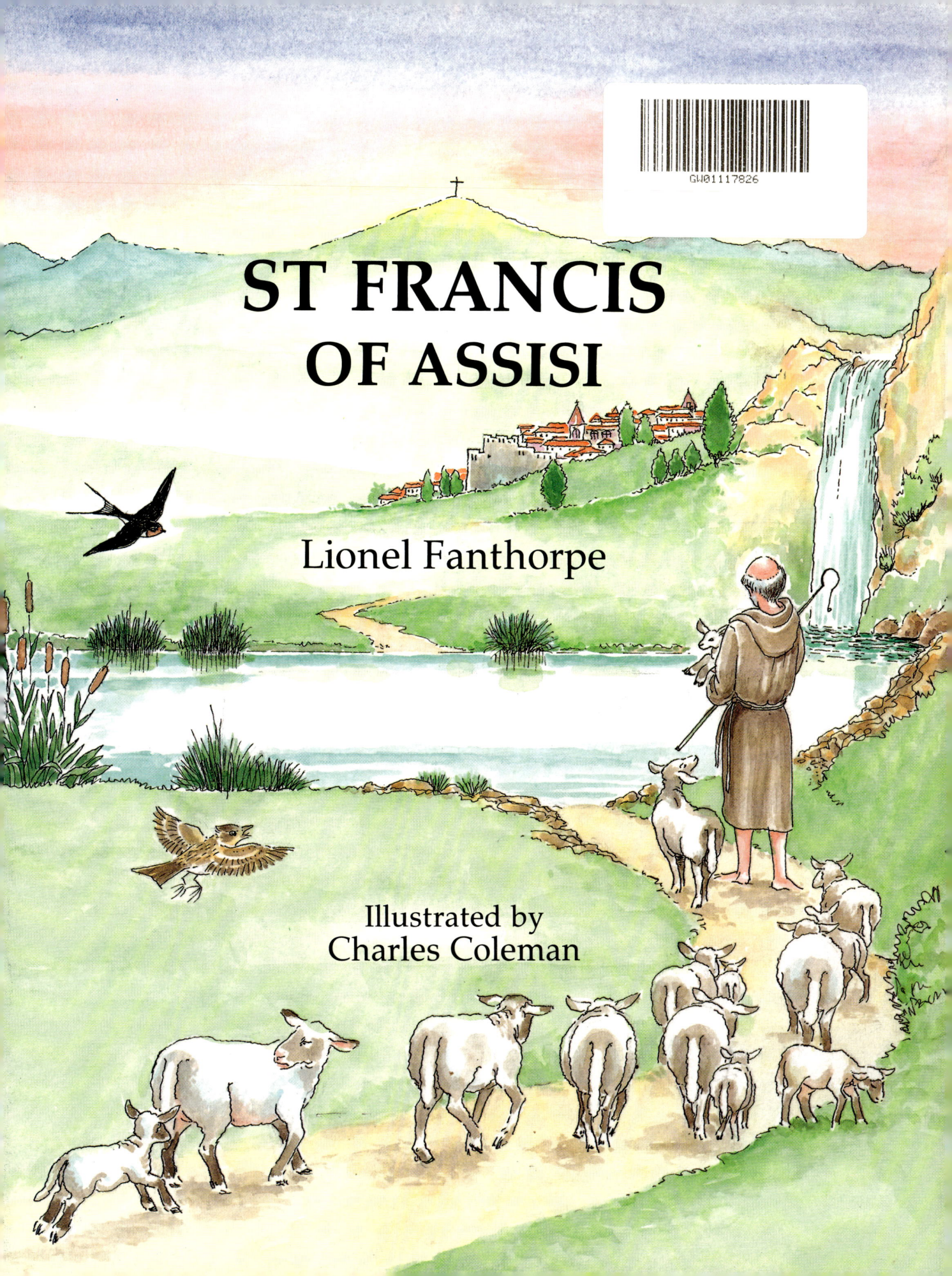

ST FRANCIS OF ASSISI

Lionel Fanthorpe

Illustrated by
Charles Coleman

In memory of my friend Francis Strong of Cardiff, who shared with his great namesake the virtues of courage, kindness, gentleness and generosity, and who made me very welcome when I was a stranger in a strange land.

... one can appreciate the truth of Archbishop Helder Camara, the great realizer of St Francis in our midst: *"No one is so poor that they cannot give, nor so rich that they cannot receive."*

Quoted from: *St Francis: A Model for Human Liberation* by Leonardo Boff, SCM Press, London.

British Library Cataloguing in Publication Data
Fanthorpe, Lionel
    The story of St. Francis of Assisi
    1. Fransciscans. Francis of Assisi, Saint
    1182 - 1226
    I. Title
    271'.3'024
    ISBN 1-85219-028-0

© (1989) Lionel Fanthorpe

All rights reserved. No part of this publication may be reproduced, stored in a retrieval system or transmitted, in any form or by any means, electronic, mechanical, photocopying, recording or otherwise, without prior permission of the copyright owner

All enquiries and requests relevant to this title should be sent to the publisher, Bishopsgate Press Ltd., 37 Union Street, London SE1 1SE.

Printed by Singapore National Printers Ltd

CONTENTS

Foreword	4
An Outline Life of St Francis	5
St Francis with God Alone	9
The Kind of Man St Francis Was	12
Some of the Things St Francis Did	24
The People St Francis Helped	26
St Francis and His Friends	29
St Francis and His Friars	30
St Francis and the Animals	31
St Francis and the Birds: St Anthony and the Fish	32

FOREWORD

by CANON S.H.MOGFORD

The author of this book and I have much in common, not least our admiration for St. Francis of Assisi, an admiration not untouched by awe. The Saint's determined poverty, the simplicity of his Faith, the embrace of his love, tend to shame us lesser mortals. He uncovers our vacillations in Faith, our love of creature comforts and our easy indignation at our fellows. Truly we are no St Francis!

The reaction of the adult, however, is not that of the young child. At that age Faith tends to be simple, love always trusting, and ideals uncompromised by experience. It is to this younger child the author introduces St Francis, who may as yet be only a name to them. He is not seeking to create young Franciscans. Such lives are only for the few. Some, however, will never lose their admiration for the Saint he here so lovingly presents.

An Outline Life of St Francis

St Francis was born in the year 1181, which was a long, long time ago. As a boy he lived with his parents in the little town of Assisi in Italy. It stands on a hillside above the valley of the River Tiber, and many pilgrims go there today just because St Francis once lived there. Pilgrims are people who go on special journeys to visit holy places and to see holy things.

St Francis' father was a rich man called Peter Bernardone. He was a merchant who bought and sold beautifully coloured woollen cloth. Because his father was rich, Francis was able to dress in expensive clothes and go to many parties with his rich friends.

As a boy, and as a young man, Francis often dreamed of how exciting it would be to become a knight in shining armour and ride off to battle on a great horse. He had heard many adventure stories about King Arthur's knights, and about another hero called Charlemagne.

While young St Francis was growing up, many wars and battles were going on in his part of Italy. The men of Perugia, a town nearby, often fought against the men of Assisi. When St Francis was a soldier in one of these battles he was taken prisoner. He became quite ill in prison and did not get home again for a whole year.

St Francis spent many hours thinking, praying and listening to God before deciding what to do next. He decided to give up all his dreams of being a knight and to give away all his money. He had made up his mind to spend his life serving God and helping people in need.

He gave away everything he had, and never again owned money or anything else except the simple clothes he wore. He felt that he could help the poor best if he became one of them himself.

During his very full life he did many good and wonderful things. He was patient, brave and kind. He was humble, generous and gentle. He was loving, forgiving and merciful. He preached the truth about Jesus, the Son of God and Saviour of the world. He taught people how to be good and happy. He spent many hours talking to God and listening to God.

He helped people to solve all kinds of problems. He helped the greedy and the selfish to think of others instead of themselves. He showed the rich how to help the poor. He taught the strong how to help the weak. He told proud and angry people that there was a much better way to live. He looked after those who were ill, or hungry. He helped those who were lost to find their way home to God.

He preached to huge crowds, and he also spoke to people who came one at a time to ask for his advice. St Francis always knew how to be a good and true friend.

St Francis loved the Church, and always did his best to serve it faithfully and keep its rules. He started a wonderful Christian Brotherhood, who are known today as the Franciscans. They do great work for God and for people in need.

He loved animals, trees and flowers, fish and birds, and there are many stories told about his unusual power over them.

St Francis died on October 3rd, 1226, and was declared a Saint on July 16th, 1230.

St Francis with God Alone

St Francis was a great man of prayer.

His spiritual power and strength came from being with God his Father in prayer as often as he could. Although Francis loved people and liked being with them to help them, he knew how important it was to be quiet and still and alone with God.

Here are some of the things he said in his prayers:-

Lord, please let me be someone You can use to bring peace to others:
where people hate each other, let me bring love instead;
where people have hurt or wronged each other, let me help them to forgive each other;
where people have doubts, let me bring them faith and true belief in You;
where there is darkness and people cannot see where to go, let me bring them Your Light;
where people have lost all their will to go on, and given up in despair, let me bring them new hope;
where people are sad and miserable, let me bring them Your Joy. Amen.

Divine Master, help me not to want other people to cheer me up and try to make me happy: help me instead to try to cheer them up and make them happy.

Help me not to think of myself and wish that other people understood me better and were kinder to me: help me instead to understand them better and be kinder to them.

Help me not to want other people to love and care for me; help me instead to love and care for them.

Teach me, Divine Master, that when we give to others we receive the greatest joy and blessing ourselves.

Teach me that when we forgive other people, we are forgiven too.

Teach me that when our selfishness and greed die, so that we put You and others before our own wants and needs, we have for the first time truly begun to live that Joyful and Eternal Life which Jesus brings for us to share. Amen.

St Francis at Prayer

St Francis was
A man of prayer,
Who knew that God
Was always there.
Beside the sea,
In field or wood,
St Francis prayed
Whene'er he could.
He turned his thoughts
To God above
And asked for grace
To make him love
The people that
He met each day,
So he could cheer
Them on their way.
Help us, dear Lord,
To pray to You,
So we can help
Our neighbours too.

The Kind of Man St Francis Was

The Patience of St Francis

St Francis loved Nature. He knew that God had created all the good, beautiful and wonderful things in the universe. Francis knew that in Nature everything had to work at its own proper speed. Seeds grew and ripened into flowers, or fruit or vegetables in their own time. Baby animals like cubs, kittens and puppies grew up slowly and naturally.

The sun rose and set, telling us when to work and when to rest and sleep.

The moon changed from new to full over and over again as it shone at night.

The tides came and went on the beach.

Spring, summer, autumn and winter all took their turns at the right time.

St Francis also knew that man was part of God's creation. He knew that men had to wait for God's proper time, if they were to serve Him well. He knew that a job had to be done slowly and carefully, if it was to be finished in the right way.

When St Francis was called by God to rebuild the broken church at San Damiano, he walked slowly and patiently up and down the streets of Assisi asking people to give him stones to mend the church.

When he had the stones, he began putting them in place with his own hands, one by one. It took a very long time.

He asked passers-by to help him, and many of them did.

Patiently, with St Francis to lead them, the people slowly mended the church.

Prayer for Patience

Dear Lord Jesus, Your servant Francis was very patient. He never gave up because he was tired or bored. He went on working for You, Your people and Your Church until his work was done.
Teach me to be like Him.
Teach me how to go on working when I feel tired or sad.
Teach me how to go on working when the job isn't very interesting.
Teach me not to grumble when I have a lot to do.
Teach me not to be lazy.
Teach me to be patient.
Teach me to be cheerful while I'm waiting.
Teach me to see that all good work is done for You, Your people and Your Church, and teach me to enjoy it. Amen.

Patience

When Francis was rebuilding
A ruined church with stone,
He worked at it so patiently;
He started all alone.
Then God sent other helpers
And so the building grew
And when their work was finished
The church was just like new.
Each job we do is like a stone
And when we've done them all
Then we shall build, as Francis built,
A strong and mighty wall.

The Courage of St Francis

Although Francis was not very big and not very strong as far as his muscles went, he was a man of very great courage. In all difficulties and dangers, his faith made him brave. He trusted God for everything, and was never afraid.

He often travelled alone, or with just one or two other Franciscans, through very dangerous country. They were in danger from robbers, from storms, from the heat and the cold. They were in danger of starving; they were in danger from thirst. They were in danger from people who became angry with them when they begged for food. There was also the risk of having an accident in the wild, lonely places they walked through.

One of the worst dangers was disease, and one of the worst diseases was leprosy. At the time when Francis lived many people suffered from it, and everyone was afraid of catching it: everyone except Francis. He was not at all afraid of it. One day when a poor leper had been made to feel sad by something that had been said, Francis sat down beside him and shared food with him. Most people would have gone as far as they could to get away from the leper.

Prayer for Courage

Dear Lord, I fear so many things:
I am afraid of other children who are big and rough;
I am afraid of the dark.
I am afraid of being alone.
I am afraid of being ill.
Sometimes I am afraid of school.
I am often afraid of getting lost.
You alone know my secret fears. I share them with You now. Please, dear Lord, make me brave, as St Francis was brave. Give me the courage that he had, so that I may try to do Your will even when it is hard.
I ask it in the name of my Lord Jesus.
Amen.

Courage

It is hard to be brave
When you're lost in the dark;
It is hard not to cry
When you get a low mark;
It is hard to be strong
When your feet want to run,
To go on when a job
That is hard *must* be done.
It is hard to hold on
When you want to let go,
When you're aching and tired,
And your body says, "No!"
Blessed Lord, make us brave,
Like St Francis of old.
He was never put off
By the heat or the cold.
He was never afraid
Of the wind or the wave:
It was trusting in You
That made Francis so brave.

The Kindness of St Francis

One of the Franciscans called Brother Masseo was a very good preacher, and was also good at many other things. St Francis was worried in case Masseo became proud of all the things that he did so well. For Masseo's own good, Francis gave him lots of extra jobs to do: he put him in charge of the door to welcome and look after all the people who called. He also put him in charge of the kitchens so that he had to prepare food and cook for all the Brothers who lived there. On top of all that work, Masseo was put in charge of helping the poor. It was far, far too much for anyone to try to do, but Masseo was a good, obedient Brother, and he tried his best to do the impossible because St Francis had told him to.

After a time the other Brothers went to see St Francis to ask him to help Brother Masseo. Francis was very pleased that they cared so much about Masseo, so he said that the work could be shared among all of them in future.

It is very hard for a man who is in charge of others, even when he is a very good man like St Francis, to change his mind once he has given an order.

In this story about Masseo we learn a lot about the nature of Francis. We learn that what he did in the first place when he gave Masseo too much work was meant to be for Masseo's own good. Francis did not give Masseo extra work because he didn't like him, but because he wanted to help him to be humble. We also learn that Francis was very willing to listen to what people said to him when they were asking for help. He was even more willing to listen when they were asking for help for someone else. Francis was so kind and good that he was happy to change his orders when changing them would help other people. He did not want what was best for him as leader, but what was best for Brother Masseo and the others.

Kindness

Lord, help me understand my brother's mind,
And, knowing how he feels, help me be kind
To him and everybody else I meet
Until I stand before Your judgement seat,
Then help me understand these words so true:
Things done to brother man are done to You.

Prayer for Kindness

Help us, Lord Jesus Christ, to be kind to everyone.
Help us to put others before ourselves and You before all.
Help us to feel what others are feeling.
Help us to see things from their point of view.
Help us to comfort the sad, and to be friends with the lonely.
Help us to support the weak, feed the hungry, heal the sick, and help all those who are in need of our help.
Help us to copy You, because Your kindness has no end, and because You are the Perfect One Whom we should always try to copy.
We ask it for Your Name's sake. Amen.

The Humility of St Francis

One day when St Francis and his friends were on a long, tiring journey, he became so weak and ill that his friends asked a poor farm worker if they could borrow his donkey for Francis to ride on. The man agreed, and they helped Francis up on to the donkey. The owner of the donkey walked behind. After a little while the man asked, "Are you Brother Francis from Assisi, the one who does so many kind things and good deeds?" Francis said that his name was Francis, and that he always tried to serve Christ and other people, but very often failed.

The man who owned the donkey looked very thoughtful for a few minutes then he spoke to Francis. "It is very important that you always do everything you can to be as good and as kind as people believe you are," he said at last, "because if you are not what they hope for, they will be very sad and feel let down. So many people have faith in you as a true man of God that you must always try hard to be one."

Francis climbed down off the donkey, and knelt at the poor man's feet. "Thank you," he said humbly, "for those wise words. You have helped me."

Humility

St Francis was a gentle man,
Not boastful, and not proud.
He honoured God and not himself
When preaching to the crowd.
If hungry folk were short of food,
Or someone had a thirst,
St Francis stood aside and let
The needy get there first.
St Francis was a humble man;
He never looked for fame.
He tried to treat the Brothers in
His Order all the same.
He knew that Jesus Christ his Lord
Had taught that leaders should
Wait on the helpless and the weak
For that's *true brotherhood*.

Prayer for Humility

Dear Lord Jesus, we are often so proud of ourselves when we should not be.
We are proud of being clever, when we are really very silly and foolish.
We think we are strong, when we are really weak and afraid.
We think we are good, when we are really selfish and unkind.
We think we are being honest, but we are not.
We think we are better than other people, when we are not.
Dear Lord Jesus, You have more reason to be proud of Yourself than anyone, but You are humble, gentle and meek.
You are the Son of God and live with Your Father in Glory,
Yet you lived with the poor when You were on earth as Man.
Help us to be humble.
Help us to think more of others than we think of ourselves.
Help us to be like Saint Francis.
Help us to be like You.
We ask it for Your Name's sake. Amen.

Some of the Things St Francis Did

Francis was a great teacher, a great preacher, a great healer and the founder of a great religious Order which still does God's work in the world today.

There are many accounts of people who were ill who came to Francis to be healed. Sometimes the Saint touched the sick person. Sometimes it was enough for the sick person just to touch something which St Francis had touched. This reminds us of the sick woman in the Gospels who had such faith in Jesus that she knew she would be healed if she could only get close enough to Him to touch the hem of His robe.

Among the great truths which Francis taught and preached were these:-

Where there is love, there will be no fear.
Where people are patient and humble, there will be no anger.
Where people fill their minds with good and peaceful thoughts about God, there will be no worries.
Where people love Christ and respect and obey His laws, no evil can enter.

Doing What St Francis Did

I want to try to *do* things —
Not stand and watch the rest.
I want to try to do things
I want to do my best.
St Francis was a *doing* man:
He healed the sick and lame.
He also preached and taught the crowds
Who gathered when he came.
He built things and he mended things;
He mended people too.
He started a great Order
Of holy men and true.
I want to be like Francis,
And be a *doing* man:
I'll ask the Lord to help me,
Then I'll do the best I can.

Prayer

Lord Jesus, help me to do things for You and for others, and
    not just to think about them, or talk about them.
Help me to be active in Your service.
Help me to do things for You.
Help me to do things for Your Church.
Help me to do things for Your people, who are my brothers
    and sisters.
I ask it in and through Your Holy Name. Amen.

The People St Francis Helped

St Francis did not only help poor people, he also helped the rich and powerful, but he helped them in a different way. Because he had once been rich himself, Francis knew how hard it was for a rich man or woman to give everything away and follow Jesus. Francis also knew that this was the way for them to find happiness. He knew all about the rich young man in the Gospels who had come to see Jesus. He was a good man who kept all God's laws, but Jesus knew at once that he would never find God, and so be truly happy, until he had got rid of the money and the many things he owned. They meant so much to him, that they stopped him from putting God first. Money is a good servant, and very useful to have, but we must never live for money. If rich people use their money to do God's will, then they are doing right. They are the masters of their money; their money has not taken charge of them.

St Francis Helps the Rich

Too much money can get in the way,
If we count it every day,
If money means more than husband or wife,
Someone is living a miser's life.
If money means more than child or friend,
Someone will come to a miser's end.
If money means more than father or mother,
Uncle or aunt, or sister, or brother,
This is the truth that we have to know:
That kind of money has got to go!
God gave us money to serve our needs,
To give us the chance to do good deeds.
A miser may scrape and scratch and save,
But he cannot spend it in his grave!
We're only the stewards of what God lends;
We must share His gifts with our poorer friends.

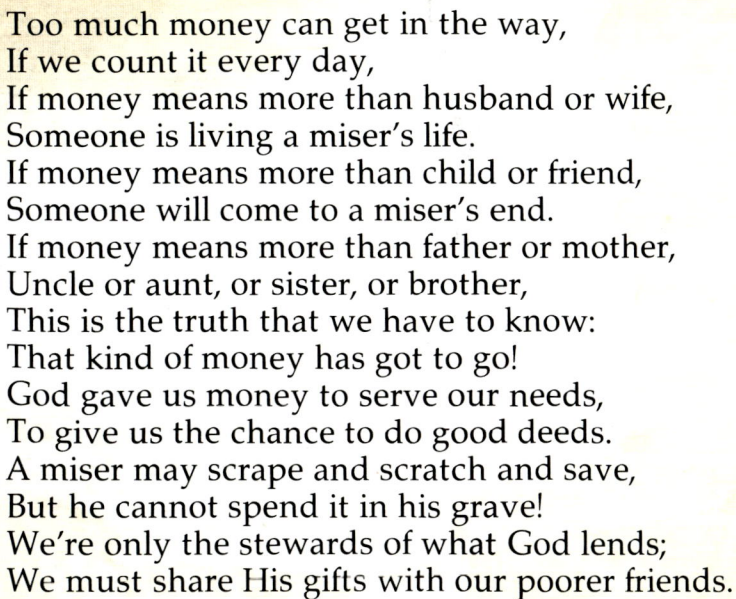

A Prayer about Money

Loving Heavenly Father,
Teach me to think about money in the right way,
The way Saint Francis thought about it,
The way Jesus, Your Son, taught men to think about it.
Help me, Lord, to remember that all wealth belongs to You.
Help me to remember that what I think of as mine is only on loan from You,
    and that I must use it properly, as You would want me to use it,
    because it is really Yours, not mine.
Help me, Lord, to see clearly that people who want money for its own sake
    are being very foolish.
Teach me to think of it as something which is here for us to
    use to help others.
Help me never to be greedy.
Help me never to be selfish.
Help me to be like Your Son, our Lord Jesus.
Help me to be like his servant, St Francis.
Help me to be generous and to enjoy giving.
Teach me that it is more blessed to give than to receive.
May I always be the happy servant of God, and never the unhappy
    servant of money.
For the sake of Jesus, my Lord and my Saviour. Amen.

St Francis and his Friends

Francis was very good at making friends and keeping them.
All kinds of people came to him and wanted to join him. Strong men came, and he told them to help the weak. Rich men came and he told them to give their money to the poor. Poor men came, and he made them very welcome. Sick men came, and he did all he could to make them well again. Lost men came, and he helped them to find God and so to find true happiness.
All these people became the friends of St Francis.

St Francis was a Friendly Man

St Francis was a friendly man,
Gentle and kind and good.
Folks told him all their troubles
And he always understood.

St Francis was a friendly man,
Who turned no one away.
He made the lonely welcome,
So he made new friends each day.

St Francis was a friendly man,
Who gave his heart and mind
To sharing everything he had
With sick, and poor and blind.

St Francis was a friendly man,
And faithful to the end.
He knew that God had called him
To be everybody's friend.

Prayer

Dear Lord Jesus, our best and most wonderful Friend,
Help us to return Your friendship to us
By being good friends to others.
We ask it for Your Name's sake. Amen.

St Francis and his Friars

One of the greatest things which St Francis did was to start a Brotherhood or Order of Friars. Our word *friar* comes from the French word *frère* which comes from the Latin word *frater* which means *brother*. St Francis's friars are called Franciscans and they still do much very good work today. They help the poor; they heal the sick; they pray; and they teach people about Jesus.

The Franciscan Friars

Franciscan Friars go out each day
Wearing a simple robe of grey.
For all the poor and sick they care,
And spend a lot of time in prayer.

Franciscan Friars are good and wise
With smiling lips and shining eyes.
The praises of their God they sing,
And share the joy of Christ, their King.

Prayer for the Franciscans

Lord Jesus, bless, help and strengthen Your Franciscans.
Help them to find the people who need their help,
And help the people who need their help to find them.
Reward them for all the good they do,
And help us always to support them
With our prayers,
With our gifts,
And by loving and serving You as they do.
For Your Name's sake. Amen.

St Francis and the Animals

There seems to have been no limit to the love which Francis had. He was as kind and gentle to animals and birds as he was to people. He felt that animals were our brothers and sisters because God had made them too. Francis knew the secret of the real link between animals and people which is made clear in the first book of the Bible: we are here to care for the animals and protect them.

Even when animals were fierce and dangerous, Francis could talk to them and make them quiet and gentle. Outside a town called Gubbio, there was a very bad wolf which frightened everyone. It attacked sheep and cattle and men and women as well.

Francis went straight up to the wolf, made the sign of the cross and said: "Come, Brother Wolf, do not harm me, and do not harm any of these people." The wolf followed Francis and became as harmless as a lamb.

Francis and the Wolf

So great was their fear,
They dared not go near:
That wolf.

Then St Francis came,
And he made it tame:
That wolf.

And before the end
It became their friend:
That wolf.

It was used to show
God's power below:
That wolf.

Prayer

O Loving Lord, Maker of all things,
Maker of men and women, boys and girls,
Maker of animals, birds and fish,
Teach us to serve You by loving and caring for all that You have made,
Through Jesus Christ our Lord. Amen.

St Francis and the Birds: St Anthony and the Fish

One day Francis and two of his friars, Brother Masseo and Brother Angelo, were at a place called Bevagna. At the spot, which is now called Pian d'Arca, St Francis saw a big flock of birds in the trees beside the road along which the three Brothers were walking. "Wait for me here," said Francis, "I will go and preach to my little sisters, the birds." And he did. He told the birds that they should sing and praise God because He had given them freedom to fly, and that He gave them everything they needed. As Francis spoke to them, the birds sat very still and seemed to be listening.

His friend St Anthony is said to have preached to the fish, and they are said to have popped their heads out of the water to listen to him.

Birds and Fishes

Men say that even the fishes and birds
Kept still to hear the holy words.
St Francis came, and St Anthony too:
"Fishes and birds — a message for you!
In the Heavens high above you
Is the Lord Who made and loves you.
He made you free; he made you strong;
He gave you the earth where we all belong.
The birds have the skies; the fish have the sea:
The land is given to men like me.
In air, or sea, or purple heather,
Let us worship God together."

Prayer

Lord of the sea and sky, Maker and Master of the land,
Accept the humble thanks and praises
Of all whom You have made.
Whether we fly or swim,
Walk, run or climb,
You have made us all and You love us all.
Help us to love You, thank You and worship You,
For the sake of Christ our Lord. Amen.